HISTORY AND THE READER

T0346162

NATIONAL BOOK LEAGUE THIRD ANNUAL LECTURE

HISTORY AND THE READER

BY

G. M. TREVELYAN
O.M.

LONDON
Published for the
NATIONAL BOOK LEAGUE
by the Cambridge University Press
1945

CAMBRIDGE
UNIVERSITY PRESS

University Printing House, Cambridge CB2 8BS, United Kingdom

Cambridge University Press is part of the University of Cambridge.

It furthers the University's mission by disseminating knowledge in the pursuit of education, learning and research at the highest international levels of excellence.

www.cambridge.org
Information on this title: www.cambridge.org/9781316611753

© Cambridge University Press 1945

First published 1945
First paperback edition 2016

A catalogue record for this publication is available from the British Library

ISBN 978-1-316-61175-3 Paperback

HISTORY AND THE READER

⁕⁕⁕⁕⁕⁕⁕

AFTER the high standard set by our President's beautiful address last year, I fear that you will find my remarks this evening somewhat pedestrian. But at any rate the subject I have chosen, "History and the Reader," raises a real question, or rather a number of real questions, on which opposite opinions have been held by people of wide and deep learning and high cultivation.

The fundamental question is whether history has any important relation to the reading public at all, or whether it is "a science, no more and no less," as was said in 1903 by Professor Bury, my predecessor in the Chair of History at Cambridge.

Bury was a scholar of very high distinction, and anything he said deserved most respectful consideration. But in 1903, as a rash young man, I ventured to controvert his definition of history as being a science and no more. I argued that it was both a science and an art: that the discovery of historical facts should be scientific in method, but that the exposition of them for the reader partook of the nature of art, the art of written words commonly called literature. More than forty years have passed since I entered upon that controversy, and I hold the same opinion still, as to the dual nature of history.

To-day it is no longer necessary to talk on this subject in a controversial tone, for historians are more eclectic and tolerant of diversities in historical methods than some of their predecessors of forty years ago. There are many living historians, finer and more truly scientific scholars than I can claim to be, who have been most generous in their attitude towards my own historical endeavours. And

7

there are a number of historical scholars who throw the results of their research into a literary form, and thereby secure the attention of a very wide public. History is no longer, as it was at the opening of this century, in the trammels of a theory that tended to make it dull. It is once more a part of the current literature of the day, often eagerly sought for by the public, though of course some historical works appeal more to the specialists, and others more to the general reader. But there is no hard and fast line between these two kinds of history.

Please, therefore, do not regard this address as part of a controversy, but only as an attempt at definition, and an enquiry into the value, or rather the values, of history to the reader.

Before approaching the question of the value of history to the general reader, I will make a few remarks on the history of history. For us Europeans, the Greek and Roman historians stand as the great originals. Herodotus and Thucydides regarded history both as a science and an art, although they may not have used that phraseology. They took great pains in collecting facts, though travel and conversation were their sources, rather than documents of which there were not many in those days. They then threw the results of what they had collected into the form of literature. Speaking under correction from classical scholars, I should imagine that we do not know how far Herodotus and Thucydides were able to arrive at all the true facts, or how far their deductions were correct. But we feel, I think, that they both sincerely sought the truth. Professor Cornford indeed argued that even Thucydides allowed his conclusions to be to some extent affected by his artistic or dramatic instincts, but this is denied by others. With Tacitus, I suppose, we feel less sure as to the impartiality of his statements, though he was pre-eminent among Roman historians in literary power. Be

8

that as it may, the tradition which Greece and Rome bequeathed to the Europe of the Renaissance was the tradition of history both as a science of facts, and as an art appealing to the general reader.

In the Middle Ages there had been some good historical work done by English monks like Matthew Paris, chiefly chronicles of contemporary events. With the Renaissance, the study of the ancient historians made modern historians more ambitious. In early Stuart times Sir Walter Raleigh solaced his captivity in the Tower by writing his monumental *History of the World*. To our generation it is unreadable, in spite of some magnificent and famous passages, but in its own day it was very widely read and exercised a great influence on the public. After that, Clarendon and Burnet carried the art of writing contemporary history to a high point. In the same era, that is in the later seventeenth century and early eighteenth century, a school of English antiquarians of great ability and zeal laid the foundation of the scientific study of the documents of the Middle Ages, in publications like those of Dugdale, Hearne, Rymer, Wake and Anthony Wood. In their work we have early examples of the scientific study of the documents of the past, which is the principal method of modern historical research.

In the middle of the eighteenth century, history in England fully developed its modern form, which has since been little changed. Three men stand out as the creators of the norm of modern historiography: Hume, Robertson and Gibbon. Gibbon is the greatest, but Hume and Robertson were his predecessors, and those two Scots have a very great place in the history of history in these islands. They made the history-reading public in Britain, which Gibbon inherited from them. In Gibbon the perfection both of the science and of the art of history were reached, and has never since been surpassed.

B

During the first three-quarters of the nineteenth century, History was regarded in England as a specialized branch of literature; history books were extensively bought and read by the large educated public of that day. Macaulay and Carlyle thought of their work as a part of the literature of their country, and their books sold as well, I believe, as those of any novelist except Dickens. But Carlyle and Macaulay were not superficial, any more than Gibbon had been superficial; they had great faults but they had not the fault of want of learning. They set a fine example by their zeal in the collection of evidence from original sources. In his *Cromwell* and his *Frederic*, Carlyle was his own Dryasdust. Macaulay's reading was stupendous. But the interpretation they put on the evidence they collected was often faulty. No doubt they lacked something of the scientific spirit in the method of collating of evidence on which so great stress was laid in the academic reaction that took place in the closing years of the century.

That reaction against "literary history," as it was scornfully called, was rampant fifty years ago, when I commenced historian. It began in the Universities and was meekly accepted by the general public as a pronouncement made *ex cathedra*. History, it was agreed, was no longer to be written for the general reader and his likes; history books were henceforth to contain only the learned talk of historians with one another. If the public sometimes overheard that talk, so much the better, but that was a matter of secondary importance. History was to have nothing to do with literature. It was a science, no less and no more. Two of my predecessors in the Chair at Cambridge loudly proclaimed this doctrine, but the two greatest Cambridge historians, Acton and Maitland, never went these doctrinal lengths, and both of them were most friendly to me and to my young hopes of writing literary history. To-day professional historians are tolerant of the diversities of historical aim in their brotherhood, and not a few of them successfully practise the art of writing literary history. And the public appears to welcome their efforts.

But the anti-literary or scientific reaction among the historians of fifty years ago, though it has now spent its force, or at least lost its intolerance, had at the time its uses and its *raison d'être*. I think it did both good and harm. I should like to summarize its principal causes.

First of all, history was at that time—half a century ago—becoming a very important subject of teaching and examination at the Universities, to some extent rivalling or even displacing Classics as the most popular "Arts" subject of general education. Now if history is to be learned and taught at the Universities, it cannot be taught as a "soft option," a branch of literature. Something rigorous like Stubbs' *Constitutional History*, and some study of the laws of historical evidence is desirable. This aspect (the scientific aspect if you like to call it so) of history was necessarily, and on the whole rightly stressed, in University teaching and study. I think Macaulay and Carlyle themselves would have been even better historians than they were, if they had been through an academic course of history such as they could have got if they had lived at the end of the nineteenth century instead of at the beginning. What was wrong with the historical reaction at the end of Victoria's reign, was not the positive stress it laid on the need for scientific method in weighing evidence, but its negative repudiation of the literary art, which was declared to have nothing whatever to do with the historian's task.

A second, and less respectable cause of the reaction, was the influence of Germany. In the last years of Victoria, Bismarck's Germany was the admired of all admirers, not least in academic circles. The American Universities, then rapidly rising in size and importance, modelled themselves not on the English but on the German example.

11

And, even in British Universities, Germany was for a while regarded as the fount whence dons and men should draw *lucem et pocula sacra*. We are always throwing over our national traditions, in every thing except politics. We have seen that happen again and again in art and in music. And so in History, fifty years ago, the English tradition of history written for the general reader, was thrown aside for the crabbed German ideal of the learned man who has nothing to do with literature.

A third cause of the "scientific" reaction in history was the predominance, prestige and success which had been attained by the physical sciences in the later years of the nineteenth century. Science had transmuted the economic and social life of mankind, and had revolutionized the religious and cosmological outlook of the educated world. These astonishing achievements of physical science led many historians, fifty years ago, to suppose that the importance and the value of history would be greatly enhanced if history was called a science, and if it adopted scientific methods and ideals and none others. I believe that this analogy was inexact. For the study of mankind does not resemble the study of the physical properties of atoms, or the life-history of animals. If you find out about one atom you have found out about all atoms, and what is true of the habits of one robin is roughly true of the habits of all robins. But the life history of one man, or even of many individual men, will not tell you the life history of other men. Moreover you cannot make a full scientific analysis of the life history of any one man. Men are too complicated, too spiritual, too various, for scientific analysis; and the life history of millions cannot be inferred from the history of single men. History, in fact, is a matter of rough guessing from all the available facts. And it deals with intellectual and spiritual forces which cannot be subjected to any analysis that can properly be called scientific.

As Carlyle wrote long ago (*Fr. Rev.* ii. 1), "Every reunion of men, is it not, a reunion of incalculable influences; every unit of it a microcosm of influences; of which how shall science calculate or prophecy?"

Moreover the value and object of history is to a very large extent—I should say mainly—to educate the public mind. But physical science has its own uses and applications quite apart from the popularizing of its results. No doubt it is desirable to popularize its results as Eddington and Jeans and more than one Huxley have done; but the main end of science is the accumulation of specialized knowledge by specialists, which can be applied to the material needs of the world.

But the chief value of history is educative, its effect on the mind of the historical student, and on the mind of the public, and therefore the business of conveying the best work and the best thought of historians to the general reader is of prime importance. That can only be done by the art of writing, so that literary skill is a part of the equipment desirable at least in some historians, though not in all. There are diversities of gifts and diversities of tasks in Clio's temple.

This brings me to the heart of my subject this evening, the question what is the value of history to the ordinary reader who is not a professional historian. Why should historians consider it a part of their business to convey their old and their new knowledge, their traditions and their discoveries, to the man in the street?

The older I get and the more I observe the tendencies and conditions of our latter day, the more certain I become that history must be the basis of humane (that is non-scientific) education in the future. Without some knowledge of history other doors will remain closed, or at best ajar. For example, the reading of poetry and prose literature, other than current books, must rest on some knowledge of the times past when the older books were written. Some understanding of the social and political scene of Chaucer's, Shakespeare's, Milton's, Swift's world, of the world of Boswell, of Wordsworth and Shelley and Byron, of Dickens and of Trollope, of Carlyle and Ruskin is necessary in order fully to appreciate the works in question, or even in some cases to understand what they are about. Music needs no such historical introduction to be fully appreciated, for it is not allusive, or only slightly. But literature is allusive; each book is rooted in the soil of the time when it was written. Unless our great English literature is to become a sealed book to the English people (as indeed I fear it is to many), our countrymen must know something of times past.

Literature and history are twin sisters, inseparable. In the days of our own grandfathers, and for many generations before them, the basis of education was the Greek and Roman classics for the educated, and the Bible for all. In the classical authors and in the Bible, history and literature were closely intervolved, and it is that circumstance which made the old form of education so stimulating to the thought and imagination of our ancestors. To read the classical authors and to read the Bible was to read at once the history and the literature of the three greatest races of the ancient world. No doubt the Classics and the Bible were read in a manner we now consider uncritical, but they were read according to the best lights of the time and formed a great humanistic education. I fear that to-day the study both of the Classics and of the Bible has dwindled to small proportions. What has taken their place? To some extent the place has been filled by a wider and more correct knowledge of history and a wider range of literature. But I fear that a great part of the lacuna has been filled up by rubbish.

14

Similarly, and only in a lesser degree than in the case of literature, the enjoyment and understanding of architecture and of painting and of all the domestic arts, are enhanced by knowledge of history. The man who knows no history can travel through Italy thinking it very pretty and picturesque and queer, but understanding very little of what he sees. Foreign travel is enjoyable and instructive largely in proportion to the amount of historical knowledge which we take with us across the Channel. But I am glad to observe that the power of enjoying old buildings by means of historical knowledge and imagination is very widely spread to-day. That is something to build on, educationally and culturally. In the years before the outbreak of the war, as many as 15,000 people every year visited Housesteads, to see Borcovicus Fort on the Roman Wall, a property of the National Trust. That is to say, 15,000 people a year, speeding along the Carlisle-Newcastle road, got out of their motor-cars or buses, or got off their bicycles, and walked half a mile uphill to inspect the ruins of some old Roman buildings on that wild moor. There is no beauty in the ruins which are little more than foundations, but the historical imagination of the visitors was touched. Some knew, more went away desiring to know, something of the history of the Romans in Britain.

The visitors to ruined abbeys and castles, to country houses and parish churches, enjoy themselves in proportion as they are equipped with historical knowledge, and with the historical imagination and curiosity that leads them to desire such knowledge. Disinterested intellectual curiosity is the life blood of real civilization.

The Anglo-Saxons, though more important than the Romans in the History of England, have left fewer monuments, for the Saxons' buildings were of wood, not of stone, except only their churches, and most of their

15

churches were replaced by lordlier structures after the Norman Conquest. So there is a tendency for the Anglo-Saxons to drop out of the popular picture of our island history. Out of sight, out of mind. Yet, even so, there is a considerable curiosity about our Saxon forefathers, a desire to know the results of the very fine work, by which the Anglo-Saxon scholars and archaeologists of the last thirty years have done so much to reveal the truth about that long and vital period in the making of England. Mr. R. H. Hodgkin's *History of the Anglo-Saxons* is an admirable example of the way in which the results of the latest scholarship, difficult and abstruse in their nature, can be made understandable and attractive to the general reader. Professor Stenton's great work on *Anglo-Saxon History*, recently published in the Oxford History of England, will appeal, perhaps, to fewer readers, but those who will apply themselves to read it will have the fascinating privilege of seeing the very pulse of the machine of scientific historical discovery at work. Mr. Hodgkin's and Professor Stenton's Anglo-Saxon histories are excellent examples of two different kinds of scholarly history, somewhat differently related to the needs of the reading public.

But the interest and value of history is very much more than the key it affords to the literature, art and monuments of the past. In itself history raises and attempts to answer two great questions—(1) what was the life of men and women in past ages? and (2) how did the present state of things evolve out of the past? The reader can be interested in the past for its own sake, for the value or instruction he finds in former states of society and former habits of thought which have passed away and left little or nothing behind. Or else the reader may be interested chiefly in the explanation which history alone can afford of the origin of the institutions, beliefs, habits and prejudices of the various peoples of the world at the present day. In other words, he can be interested in the past, either for its own sake, or as the parent of the present. Similarly, he may be interested in static views of various past scenes and happenings, or he may be interested principally in the moving stream of events, the causal and evolutionary aspect of the history of mankind.

I will say a little about these two aspects of history separately. First, the value to the reader of discovering what life was like in various ages and countries of old: this kind of intellectual curiosity can in our day be satisfied more fully and more correctly than in any previous age, because of the wonderful work of modern scholarship. It is a relief to escape from our own mechanical age into a world when the craftsman was more and the machine less, when imagination was more and science was less. Nor is this mere hedonistic escapism. It enlarges the mind and imagination, otherwise imprisoned in the present. We get glimpses of other worlds, human and faulty like ours, but different from our own, and suggesting many things, some of great value, that man has thought, experienced and forgotten. Indeed, I know of no greater triumph of the modern intellect than the truthful reconstruction of past states of society that have been long forgotten or misunderstood, recovered now by the patient work of archaeologists, antiquarians and historians. To discover in detail what the life of man on earth was like a hundred, a thousand, ten thousand years ago is just as great an achievement as to make ships sail under the sea or through the air.

How wonderful a thing it is to look back into the past as it actually was, to get a glimpse through the curtain of old night into some brilliantly lighted scene of living men and women, not mere creatures of fiction and imagination, but warm-blooded realities even as we are. In the matter of reality, there is no difference between past and present; every moment a portion of our prosaic

17   C

present drops off and is swallowed up into the poetic past.

The motive of history is at bottom poetic. The patient scholar, wearing out his life in scientific historical research, and the reader more idly turning the pages of history, are both enthralled by the mystery of time, by the mutability of all things, by the succession of the ages and generations.

The best expression of the sense of poetry in the annals of the past was given by Carlyle, in his *French Revolution*, his *Past and Present* and his Essay of *Boswell's Johnson*.

"History after all," he writes, "is the true poetry; Reality, if rightly interpreted, is grander than Fiction; nay even, in the right interpretation of Reality and History, does genuine Poetry lie.

Thus for *Boswell's Life of Johnson* has Time done, is Time still doing, what no ornament of Art or Artifice could have done for it. Rough Samuel and sleek wheedling James *were*, and *are not*. Their Life and whole personal Environment has melted into air. The Mitre Tavern still stands in Fleet Street: but where now is its scot-and-lot paying, beef-and-ale loving, cocked-hatted, pot-bellied Landlord; its rosy-faced assiduous Landlady, with all her shining brass-pans, waxed tables, well-filled larder-shelves; her cooks and bootjacks, and errand boys and watery-mouthed hangers-on? Gone! Gone! The becking Waiter, who, with wreathed smiles, was wont to spread for Samuel and Bozzy their supper of the gods, has long since pocketed his last sixpence; and vanished, sixpences and all, like a ghost at cock-crowing. The Bottles they drank out of are all broken, the Chairs they sat on all rotted and burnt; the very Knives and Forks they ate with have rusted to the heart, and become brown oxide of iron, and mingled with the indiscriminate clay. All, all has vanished; in very deed and truth, like that baseless fabric of Prospero's air-vision. Of the Mitre Tavern nothing but the bare walls remain there; of London, of England, of the World, nothing but the bare walls remain; and these also decaying (were they of adamant), only slower. The mysterious River of Existence rushes on; a new Billow thereof has arrived, and lashes wildly as ever round the old embankments; but the former Billow with its loud, and eddyings, where is it?—Where?—

Now this *Book* of Boswell's, this is precisely a revocation of the edict of Destiny; so that Time shall not utterly, not so soon by several centuries, have dominion over us. A little row of Naphtha-lamps, with its line of Naphtha-light, burns clear and holy through the dead Night of the Past: they who are gone are still here; though hidden they are revealed, though dead they yet speak. There it shines, that little miraculously lamp-lit Pathway; shedding its feebler and feebler twilight into the boundless dark Oblivion, for all that our Johnson *touched* has become illuminated for us: on which miraculous little Pathway we can still travel and see wonders" (*Critical Essays*, 4).

Such is the value of biography and of all history.

So, too, the finest thing ever said about the French Revolution was also said by Carlyle.

"The Fireship is old France, the old French Form of Life; her crew a Generation of men. Wild are their cries and their ragings there, like spirits tormented in that flame. But, on the whole, are they not *gone*, O Reader? Their Fireship and they, frightening the world, have sailed away; its flames and its thunders quite away, into the Deep of Time. One thing therefore History will do: pity them all; for it went hard with them all" (*French Revolution*, iii. 2).

We, I think, can appreciate that figure, sailing away as we are, on our own burning fireship, "into the Deep of Time."

Besides the contemplation and study of the Past for its own sake, there remains the second great value of History, namely the light it throws on the present. You cannot understand your own country, still less any other, unless you know something of its history. You cannot even understand your own personal opinions, prejudices and emotional reactions unless you know what is your heritage as an Englishman, and how it has come down to you. Why does an Englishman react one way to a public or private situation, a German another way, a Frenchman in a third way? History alone can tell you.

In this stage of the world, when many nations are brought into close and vital contact for good and evil, it is essential, as never before, that their gross ignorance of one another should be diminished, that they should begin to understand a little of one another's historical experience and resulting mentality. It is a fault of the English to expect the people of other countries to react as they do themselves to political and international situations. Our genuine good will and good intentions are often brought to nothing, because we expect other people to be like ourselves. This would be corrected if we knew their history, not necessarily in detail but in broad outlines of the social and political conditions which have given to each nation its present character.

You cannot understand the French unless you know something of the French Revolution, its causes and effects; or the Germans (who, bad as they are, have got to be explained and realized), without knowing something of the historical relation of the German to his government, and of the German government to the Army, and of the

20

whole nation to military ideals, as potent and precious to them as Parliamentary institutions (and freedom to do whatever we like) have, in the long course of history, become to us English. You cannot understand the Russians, unless you have some conception of the long centuries during which they were hammered into the sense of community by the continual blows of Tartar and Teuton invasion sweeping over the unbroken Steppes. We are always expecting other countries to "Play the game" as we play it, to see life as we see it, and when they do not we are surprised and helpless. The present is always taking us by surprise (as it did in 1938–9) because we do not sufficiently know and consider the past.

Mr. Ford, it is commonly reported, once declared that history was "bunk." This remarkable utterance of his, if indeed he made it, was in itself an outcome of history: such contempt for all things past, and such engaging frankness in avowing it, were themselves the outcome of certain aspects of the social history of the United States in the nineteenth century. Yet the American, generally speaking, is by no means ignorant of history or uninfluenced by his knowledge of it. The Americans know more about our history than we know about theirs, though I hope that will soon be remedied. And the American's conception of his own country, his pride in the star-spangled banner, and in the constitution, and in America as the representative of freedom and of democracy, are products of history as popularly taught and conceived over there. His attitude towards Britain, both in its favourable and in its unfavourable aspect, is largely an outcome of historical reading and teaching.

There is, indeed, another political danger that arises out of imperfect historical knowledge. I mean the danger that comes, not from deliberate propaganda or falsification, but from learning bits of past history without bringing the

21

story up to recent and present times. The Americans, for example, tend to think of England as she was long ago, as a monarchical and aristocratic country. Their knowledge of our past is greater than their knowledge of our present. A few months ago, a friendly and intelligent American officer said to me that when he first came over to England for this war he expected to find a land of castles with serfs tilling the soil for the benefit of a feudal aristocracy. I told him that his historical knowledge of England would have been suitable if he had come over to lend a hand in the *earlier* part of the Hundred Years War.

Some nations, like the Irish, are *too* historically minded, in the sense that they cannot get out of the past at all. And many of the countries of Eastern Europe, and above all the Germans themselves, have been brought up on one-sided, ultra-patriotic versions of things past. The harm that one-sided history has done in the modern world is immense. When history is used as a branch of propaganda it is a very deadly weapon. On the whole, that is not a fault of history as it is now taught and written in England. It is rather the ignorance of history than the misuse of it, from which we suffer in this island now.

Professor Butterfield, in his inaugural lecture for the Chair of Modern History at Cambridge, said last winter:

"Nations do remember one thing and another in the past. And so terrible are the evils of a little history that we must have more history as quickly as we can. And since one of the most dangerous devices of propaganda at the present day—by far the neatest trick of the year—is to narrate what the foreigner once did, while withholding everything in the nature of historical explanation, we must have more of the kind of history which is not mere narrative but exposition—the history which takes account of the differences between the centuries, between stages of intellectual development, even between types of social structure. The study of history matters, not because it turns men into statesmen—that at least is a thing which it palpably does not do (valuable though it may be when added to the other qualifications of a political leader)—but because in every genuine victory that it gains, it is contributing to the growth of human understanding."

These words of Professor Butterfield lead us on from consideration of history as a means of acquiring positive knowledge, to history as an education of the mind of the reader. We become wiser—less foolish at any rate—if we study the problems of humanity in past ages, because we can read without violent *parti-pris* about the things of long ago, and with knowledge of their outcome and consequence. It is still too early to form a final judgment on the French Revolution, and opinions about it (my opinion certainly) is constantly oscillating. On such great and complex issues there can never be a final "verdict of history." But at least it is more possible to have an opinion of some value about the French Revolution now than it was in 1789, 1794 or 1815. And the attempt to form such an opinion in all the historical light now available, is an education to the mind, the sort of education we all most terribly need.

Our own daily affairs, political and social, we approach with strong prejudices, with ignorance or onesided knowledge of the issues, and with no knowledge at all of what is going to be the outcome. To remedy this, the reading of history instils into us the habit of surveying broadmindedly and calmly the pageant and process of human affairs. I do not mean that we should be "impartial" in the sense of thinking that all sides in the past were equally in the right. We may, and we often should, feel that one side was on the balance much more in the right than the other. And we shall not all of us come to the same conclusions on these past problems. But if we calmly study the past from as many angles as possible, we shall all of us gain in wisdom and understanding. We shall acquire a mentality which, when we return to our own problems, will be less at the mercy of newspapers and films, trying to make us take short cuts to truth, and to oversimplify the tangled skein of human affairs.

I hope I have begun to make out to your satisfaction my case for the twin proposition, (1) that it is part of the duty of historians to present history in a readable form, or rather, in a variety of forms readable by various sections of the public; for in Clio's house are many mansions; And (2) that the general reader ought to study history. If he knows no history he is not properly educated either as a citizen or as an intellectual and imaginative being. But of course few readers will study history because they think it a patriotic duty to do so, or even because they want to improve their minds. Readers read because they like reading, and the books they choose will be those that interest or delight them. People will read history if it fascinates them. It is therefore the duty of historians to make it as fascinating as possible, or at any rate not to conceal its fascination under the heap of learning which ought to underlie but not overwhelm written history.

And how fascinating history is—the long, variegated pageant of man's still continuing evolution on this strange planet, so much the most interesting of all the myriads of spinners through space. Man's evolution is far more extraordinary than the first chapter of Genesis used to lead people to suppose. Man's history, pre-historic, ancient, mediaeval and modern, is by far the most wonderful thing in the Universe of which any news has come through to us. It contains religion; it contains science; at least it contains their history. It contains art and literature. The story of man is far more wonderful than the wonders of physical science. It is a mystery unsolved, yet it is solid fact. It is divine, diabolic—in short, human. "The proper study of mankind is man," more proper to him than even the study of beetles, of gases, and of atoms. And this wonderful pageant can be viewed both in rapidly revolving films of large expanses of time and space, and in "close-ups" of single people and single scenes.

What then is the likelihood that history will in fact fill the place it should fill in the national literature of to-day and to-morrow? In some respects the prospects are good. Historians often make a conscious effort to present their work to the general public in a readable form. And correspondingly a considerable interest in history is shown by large sections of the community at large. There is a demand for history books.

But I am bound to add that there is a less favourable side to the picture. In the first place there is likely to be a shortage of historians, because the weight of this long war has fallen on the students of arts subjects, including history. Science men and mathematicians were allowed by Government to come up to the University for two years before going into the fighting forces, and when they were in the forces they could for the purposes of the war carry on, to a greater or less extent, their professional training. But historical students have been debarred from the Universities for the duration, and when they are in the fighting forces they cannot study history, in the way that a Sapper, for instance, continues to enlarge his engineering knowledge, or a medical officer his knowledge of medicine. For years past hardly any young historians have been trained. What proportion of the potential historians who have missed their University education, will return alive from the war, and what proportion of the survivors will be able or willing to come to the Universities after long years of military service? I do not know. I only know that you will not get history if there are no historians.

That is one danger that faces history. Another is the difficulties in getting history books reprinted. The study of history depends more than any other branch of science or literature on the availability of a large number of books.

The present book shortage which today debars the ordinary reader to a large extent from the study of history, is I fear, not going to come to an end in a night now that the enemy have surrendered. The present acute stage, due to the paper shortage will gradually be remedied, though very gradually, I fear. But even when paper is again plentiful, modern conditions will not be favourable to the supply of history books. This was already so before the war, and will be still more so in the future. The production of books, owing to the rising cost of printing and binding, gets more and more expensive, with the result that publishers cannot reprint old books of standard value, such for example as Lecky's *Histories*—I could give fifty other other cases of good history books that are thus suffered to die. There is always a certain demand for them, but not enough to repay the costs of re-publication. Now the study of history depends on the reading of good old books, both primary sources and secondary narratives. If the reading public can in future buy nothing but the books of the day, its historical reading and knowledge will be a very poor affair.

The demand for standard histories and historical sources of ten, thirty or a hundred years ago is not great enough to pay for their re-publication. One reason why the demand is not great enough to encourage publishers to re-publish, is the disappearance of the private library. Private libraries of many different kinds and sizes were among the best things in the Victorian civilization. I fear they are disappearing and not being replaced. It is partly a result of reduced incomes, partly of the reduced size of houses. In the brave new world of the near future, our one-class society will be housed in small houses where there is little room for bookshelves. And when the motor car and its petrol are paid for there will be little money left over for books. Of course, the increase of public libraries and circulating libraries will be some compensation. But it will not fill the gap.

But I do not wish to end on a note of pessimism. The new civilization will no doubt find means of meeting its own problems, if it can succeed in avoiding world wars. And in so far as the higher civilization can manage to survive, I have no doubt that history will play a greater part than ever before in the humanistic or non-scientific aspects of culture. History is not the rival of Classics or of modern literature, or of the political sciences. It is rather the house in which they all dwell. It is the cement that holds together all the studies relating to the nature and achievements of man.